# THE QUICK EXPERT'S GUIDE TO

## Safe Social Networking

### Anita Naik

WAYLAND
www.waylandbooks.co.uk

First published in 2014 by Wayland

Copyright © Wayland 2014

Wayland
338 Euston Road
London NW1 3BH

Wayland Australia
Level 17/207 Kent Street
Sydney, NSW 2000

Editor: Nicola Edwards
Design: Rocket Design (East Anglia) Ltd
All images and graphic elements: Shutterstock

Consultant: Holly Seddon, editor-in-chief of Quibly,
which offers innovation and inspiration to modern parents.
www.quib.ly

A catalogue record for this book is available from the British
Library
Dewey number: 302.3'0285-dc23

ISBN  978 0 7502 8106 5
Library ebook ISBN: 978 0 7502 8559 9

Printed in China

Wayland is a division of Hachette Children's Books,
an Hachette UK company

www.hachette.co.uk

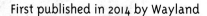

# >>>CONTENTS<<<

We have highlighted blogs, websites and tools throughout this guide in bold; we didn't want to overload you with URLs, but you should be able to find them really easily through search engines.

# TO THE UTTERLY EXCELLENT GUIDE TO SAFE SOCIAL NETWORKING!

Social networking — let's face it, who doesn't know about Facebook, Twitter, Instagram and all the apps used to network and post everything from pictures to video? You're probably online right now, on your phone, a computer, a tablet or even games console. Perhaps you're posting selfies, gossiping with friends, or ranting about who's annoyed you and why. And if you're not 'networking' yet, the chances are you and your mates soon will be.

**So, why a guide to social networking?** Well, right now social networks are getting blamed for everything from bullying to antisocial behaviour, sexism and more. But we're here to show you that being part of a network can be a positive experience. Aside from the fact they are incredibly good fun (doing everything from making you laugh to helping you feel closer to friends), they can be an amazing source for good. Through them you can show your support for causes, help change the law and even support people who you feel need your help.

**Of course, there's the down side;** peer pressure, privacy issues, online nastiness and even stranger danger and online grooming, but this guide will show you how to navigate all of that just as you have to in the real world.

## SO GET ON BOARD AND DISCOVER HOW YOU CAN ENJOY SAFE SOCIAL NETWORKING WITH THE QUICK EXPERT TEAM'S SHOW-AND-TELL ON:

The low-down on making **privacy settings** work for you

**Top tips** for keeping your **friends** close and **bullies** away

The best ways to avoid **peer pressure** and **stranger danger**

Content-sharing **dos** and **don'ts**

Managing your **online life** and making your **voice heard**

# WHAT IS SOCIAL NETWORKING?

## ✻ SOCIAL MEDIA AND SOCIAL NETWORKING: WHAT'S THE DIFFERENCE?

To many of us social media and social networking are names for one and the same thing — the sites and apps that we are social on. So while this incorporates the big guns like Facebook, Instagram and Twitter it also includes pupil/teacher sites, app review sites such as FourSquare and specialist social networking sites like LinkedIn.

However, if you want to be techie about it there is a clear difference between social media and social networks and the way they are used. Social Media is an outlet for broadcasting (YouTube, Instagram) and is made for sharing and discussing information watched and seen. While Social Networking sites (LinkedIn, Twitter) are used for connecting with others for a variety of reasons.

SAY WHAT?

SOCIAL NETWORKING IS THE SECOND MOST POPULAR ONLINE ACTIVITY IN THE WORLD. Globally, 1 in every 5 minutes is spent on social networking sites.

Of course, there is a huge crossover here as you can literally do both on each site, with the very big sites like Twitter and Facebook being both social media and social networking sites where you can share and discuss media while connecting to other people.

Right now there are over 300 social media sites/apps, with over 100 million active users. This means there's a community for everyone, with nearly all interests covered.

## HISTORY OF SOCIAL NETWORKING SITES

- Though people argue the point, it's thought social networks started with the BBS (Bulletin Board System) online meeting places in the late 1980s.

- The true ancestors to today's social networking sites were the early member portal communities like AOL (America Online) way back in the early 1990s. These member sites allowed users to list details about themselves and link to other members on the portal.

- This was followed by the emergence of websites such as Friends Reunited (UK) and Classmates.com (US), which encouraged us all to connect with old friends. Yet it was the emergence of Friendster and MySpace that really brought social networks into focus and of course the arrival of Facebook that made social networking a commonplace online activity.

# * WHAT ARE THE SOCIAL NETWORKING SITES?

Facebook, Twitter, YouTube, Pinterest and Instagram are just some of the currently popular (because they change all the time) huge social networking sites and apps. Basically, these connect people and enable them to create large networks in order to do everything from share pictures to chat about school and work.

Like anything, social networks (even the big ones) fall in and out of favour. Take the once huge Friends Reunited and MySpace, which have now been usurped by Facebook and Twitter. Of course, some sites completely capture people's imagination to the point that they couldn't imagine life without them. Facebook, for instance is a phenomenon in itself with a population so big (1.4 billion) that if it were a country, it would be the world's third largest! Having said that, the latest research shows Facebook falling out of favour with teens, and the use of instant anonymous social networking apps becoming increasingly popular.

https://en-gb.facebook.com/ElizabethTheSecond

SAY WHAT?

Even The Queen has an official Facebook page.

You may think that you will only ever have the time to be on one social network, but the reality is that most people eventually juggle a number of networks. So here's a list of the major social networking sites/apps to be aware of, with a quick description of how each works.

◔ Twitter: I am eating a pizza (sharing what you're doing right now)

◔ Facebook: Here's why I like pizza (sharing info about yourself)

-  Instagram: Here is my pizza (sharing visuals of your life as it's happening)

- YouTube: Watch me eat a pizza (sharing a video short of you eating pizza)

- Tumblr: Check out all these pictures of pizzas I like (sharing your love of pizza)

- Pinterest: Here are recipes, pictures and pretty stuff about pizza (sharing your obsession with pizza)

# ✳ EXPLAINING THE MAIN NETWORKS

While each social network works differently, it's worth knowing that many sites are designed to do the same thing. They collect information about you, and then allow you to talk — via a profile page — with a huge range of people that you then pull into your network. It's a bit like renting a huge room (your profile page) from a landlord (the social networking site) and then inviting as many people as you know — and some you don't know — (your followers and friends) to come into that room and chat to you and all your friends in any way they want, while also being given access to their rooms (profiles) and their networks (friends and followers).

Whichever network you join, it's important to remember that many are integrated with Facebook. This means if you connect through Facebook onto a new social network (for example, if you don't key any information and just log in using your Facebook account) the site you're joining will post to Facebook on your behalf. This means that, unless you change your settings (more on that later in chapter 3), whatever you do on this social networking site will automatically appear on Facebook. So which network should you join? The next few pages will tell you all you need to know.

https://en-gb.facebook.com

**Facebook**. Who hasn't heard of Facebook? It's the world's largest social networking site with over 1.4 billion users. To be a part of Facebook you need to be 13 years old and register on the site with a fair bit of information about yourself. And while it's possible to slip under the net and join before you're 13 (by changing your DOB) do be aware that Facebook has some pretty adult content, hence its age restriction.

SAY WHAT?

There are around 12 million teens under 13 years old active on Facebook.

Once you're on Facebook the aim is to create a personal profile and then start connecting and increasing your network by adding friends, friends of friends, and family. Alongside this you then interact with your network by posting status updates about yourself in a variety of different forms: messages, emoticons (such as smiley faces), photos, videos and news stories. You can then go on to comment, tag pictures, private message and interact with anyone in your network.

The downside? Well, if you use it correctly with the right privacy settings (again, see chapter 3), you'll be fine. However, many people are follower obsessed, which means they're so eager to get as many Facebook friends as possible that they link up with anyone who asks. This then means that people you don't know end up having access to a lot of your life.

That said, Facebook is the Rolls Royce of the social networking world. It's been a huge force for good, championing causes and even helping to change the law and petition for everything from ending child labour to stamping out everyday sexism.

**YouTube.** If you fancy watching a funny video, seeing your favourite band's latest interview or music video, YouTube is the place to go. Right now it's the world's second-largest search engine after Google and, like any social network, it is a mixed bag. Here you'll find a wealth of funny, amazing and clever stuff designed to make you laugh and think, and a great majority of the clips are worth sharing and commenting on. It's a great place to get behind causes you believe in and open other people's eyes to issues you believe are important. However, YouTube also has a huge amount of adult content, much of which is scary, violent and offensive. So be careful what you click on in searches, and be careful what your friends share with you.

www.youtube.com

**Twitter.** Up until recently, Twitter was seen as an adult site that didn't hold much for teens. Yet new research shows more and more teens signing up and getting involved in the conversation. Twitter, for those who don't know, is basically a social networking site that allows the user to send text-based messages of up to 140 characters, known as tweets. The length of the message means you have to be short and sharp about what you're saying.

https://twitter.com

Twitter also allows you to join in Twitter conversations with anyone you're following. And you can follow anyone you like — from celebrities to pop stars (though you can only 'direct message' people who are following you and vice versa). Twitter is also one of the social networks that has done much to campaign against wrongs, especially those in the press, and given a voice to those who don't feel they have a platform to say things. Twitter has 500 million users.

www.tumblr.com

**Tumblr**. This is a mirco blogging social networking site where users can share information of topics that are important to them. There are blogs here on education, music, pop bands and food (to name but a few) that are made up of video, images and short posts. Most of the people on Tumblr are aged 14 to 25 and the site boasts 108.4 million blogs and 216 million monthly users. Tumblr (like many social networks and apps) has its share of dark corners, so it pays to be careful when searching for topics and other users. Be careful with your use of hashtags or you may find yourself looking at inappropriate content.

http://instagram.com

**Instagram.** You can use this app to share photos from your life. Due to the nature of Instagram you can either just stay here or simultaneously upload your photos to a number of social networks synced to your Instagram account. There are currently 130 million users on Instagram, so privacy settings are very important. All photos you take (especially on smartphones) are what is known as geo-tagged — this means your location comes up with the picture). So you should turn off Geo-Tagging/Location-based services for Instagram accounts.

http://ask.fm

**Ask.Fm.** Who hasn't heard of ASK recently? It's probably the most infamous of social networking apps/sites and for a very good reason. This is a social media site where you can choose to be anonymous and post questions and responses (in 300 characters) to other people's queries. This has led to the site being linked with a lot of bullying and nastiness, as users can take advantage of the anonymous part of the equation to say pretty much whatever they like. Plus, Ask.fm is has no parental controls but more than 60 million users.

www.skype.com/en/

**Skype.** This fulfils many of the same functions as Facebook, Twitter and other sites. You can set a status 'mood' message, send a text message, use it as a group chat system, share files and photos and you can talk with people and make video calls. Plus you can connect to anyone who asks you, which means you may not know who you're dealing with. Skype currently has 300 million users.

**Pheed.** This is a new social media platform that lets you share text, photos, videos and audio. With one million users it's one of the biggest networks for teenagers, with a user base of 81% between the ages of 14 and 25.

**Pinterest.** If you're a visual type of person you will love the social network Pinterest, which is a bit like having a scrapbook online. Currently 70 million users create boards of their favourite images and then share the images with others. You can use your own pictures or almost any picture you come across.

**LinkedIn.** Until recently LinkedIn was restricted to adults and had 238 million users, but the age restriction has now been lowered from 18 to 13 years. LinkedIn is a professional social network that people use to network for jobs. It's different from Facebook and all the other social networks as its aim is to help users differentiate between the public profile they want for employment and the one they have for friends and family.

**Edmodo**. This is a new social network designed to connect students and teachers online. It offers an interface similar to that of Facebook, and anyone can post articles, videos or questions to groups. It has 18 million users, and is designed for teachers who sign up for the service for free, then add their students to the website. Using the network, teachers can write messages about assignments, post related materials for assignments or discuss a topic from class. All these updates are viewed in a Facebook-style stream of information. What happens if you use the site for non-academic purposes? Teachers can delete comments.

**Little Gossip**. This is a fast-growing social networking site that you have to be 18 to enter. All users are anonymous but the site has a number of younger users who are attracted to the fact it's all about posting and rating gossip.

www.pheed.com

www.pinterest.com

https://uk.linkedin.com

www.edmodo.com

www.littlegossip.com

## >> THE BOFFIN BIT <<

### WHY IS FACEBOOK SO SUCCESSFUL?

Aside from being easy to use and simple to set up, the key to the success of Facebook is its 'Like' button, which now appears all over the internet. This allows the user to rate anything they 'like' from virtually any other site on their profile page and makes the promoters of every brand, person and product want them to be on Facebook.

The other thing Facebook does better than any other social network is to entice users to share, and helps them to do so in a very quick and simple way. Whether it's simply telling people where they are (geo-tagging place button) or what they like (the like button) or even how they feel (emoticons).

The Facebook log-in, which allows people a short cut to log in to other sites (i.e. you log on via Facebook rather than having to key all your info in again and again) is yet another reason why people love Facebook (though it's also possible to log into a variety of sites with Twitter and LinkedIn).

However, probably the biggest reason why Facebook is so appealing is that it allows us all to catch up with friends, long-lost friends and family with minimal effort and make social arrangements quickly. No long phone calls, no meet ups and no having to write and send long emails.

https://vine.co

**Vine.** Another video sharing app, where the idea is to take a short video, upload it to Vine, share it on Facebook, and it goes out publicly. There have been problems with some inappropriate content, abusive comments and rude videos on Vine, though you can report offensive content.

**Keek**. This social network allows users to upload video status updates, called 'keeks', using a webcam or via the Keek mobile apps. Users can also reply with text or video comments, known as 'keekbacks', and share content to other major social media networks. As for many social networks, the danger here is that anyone can subscribe to your updates, view all their content and find out where you live through Geo Location. Plus there are no privacy settings or restrictions on adult content.

www.keek.com

**FourSquare**. Foursquare is a location-based social network app. The idea is, when you're out and about you can use Foursquare to share, rate and save the places you visit. You 'check in' to a location, such as a restaurant, recording your position on a map for friends using the service to see. The more often you check in, the better your chances of being declared the 'mayor' of a particular location. The obvious downside is that you are revealing exactly where you are.

https://foursquare.com

# THE RISE OF SOCIAL MESSAGING APPS

While it's hard to see the power of Facebook ever waning, recent research shows there has been an exodus by many teens from the main social media sites towards social messaging apps, thanks in part to the fact that most of us now network via smartphones.

Even though Facebook and Twitter have app versions, messaging apps like WhatsApp, SnapChat and Instagram are racing ahead of the social network as they offer something different from the more public space of Facebook (though Facebook does also have a messaging service). For a start these apps allow you to take part in real-time chatting with a group of friends you select and also to have private conversations.

What's more, although these are called messaging apps they are in fact social networks because, like Facebook, on some of them you can share everything from music and video to games and of course endless chat.

Research shows that social messaging apps play a massive part in the social lives of many of us and it's worth remembering that many of the messages about staying safe around social networks apply to apps in exactly the same way.

# IMPORTANT THINGS TO KNOW ABOUT SOCIAL NETWORKS

There are some vital things to know about social networks before you start using them. The most important of these is that social networks are more influential than you might think. This means that whatever you say, show and post on these sites can have a huge impact in your world. Not only is the information shared faster than you could ever imagine, but it also tends to have a long shelf life. This means you need to be very careful about what you say and do online, as somewhere down the line a future employer or college may google you to see what they can find (this is already happening in the USA).

Secondly, networks by their design encourage you to share. So when we're deciding how much information to reveal, many of us do not exercise the same amount of caution as we would in real life because

❂ **The lack of physical interaction provides a false sense of security.**

❂ **We tend to tailor the information for friends to read, forgetting that others may see it too.**

❂ **We forget how many people we're 'talking' to and who is watching.**

❂ **We think the information we're giving is private and haven't checked the privacy settings.**

Thirdly, legitimate social networking sites (and not all are) will have a privacy statement which tells you how they collect and use your information and when and how they might disclose this information either through the website or to third parties. These policies can change, so it's important to keep checking how much information you reveal in your profile.

*DIY DUDE*

Before you sign up...

Whenever you sign up for games/polls/apps inside a social network, read the individual privacy policy. Don't assume that they will have the same policy as the network you are currently on.

Remember, it's the quality not the size of your network that counts in social networking. Having 3000 friends or followers is a waste of time if your timeline (the information you see when you're on the social network) is clogged up with photos and comments from people you don't know and don't want to know. Which means when creating your network it pays to be selective.

Dude!

# QUICK EXPERT SUMMARY

- Social media and social network sites are sites where you can connect with people, friends and family and share any type of information.

- Information shared on social networks range from personal details to status updates, photos, videos and more.

- You don't have to belong to all the main social networks, but many are integrated (linked).

- There is pretty much a social network for everything, from looking for work, to sharing pictures and photos. But not all social networks are made equal; know what you're getting into before you sign up.

- All social networks are open to abuse, so watch your privacy settings and think about what you are sharing.

# WHO'S ON SOCIAL MEDIA?

## ✳ WHO'S NETWORKING AND WHAT ARE THEY DOING?

Does it feel like the whole world is on social networks? Well if it does, that's because they are. One centre in the USA has been studying the use of online social networking sites since 2005. The study, known as the Pew Research Centre's Internet & American Life Project, has found that 72% of online adults use social networking sites. Although younger adults continue to be the most likely social media users, one of the more striking growth areas are those aged 65 and older who have roughly tripled their presence on social networking sites in the last four years — from 13% to 43%.

That said, a recent study from the University of Winchester and the First Direct bank showed that how we behave on social networks really depends more on our personalities than our age groups. Here are the 12 types of social media behaviour identified in the study:

**The Ultras** These people are obsessed with Facebook or Twitter. They have smartphone apps and check their feeds dozens of times a day — even while they're at school or at work. The survey revealed that 14% of Facebook users spend at least two hours a day on the network — rising to one in five (21%) of 18- to 24-year-olds.

**The Deniers** Although they may claim not to be addicted to social media, if social networks were taken away from these people they'd become agitated upset and angry. They are also the people most likely to spend more time online talking to you than talking to you in person.

*The survey found that one fifth (20%) of Facebook users and 17% of Twitter users would feel 'anxious' or 'isolated' if their accounts were deactivated.*

**The Dippers** Although more than half the UK population is signed up to social networks like Facebook or Twitter, not all use them regularly. 'Dippers' access their pages infrequently, often going for days or even weeks without a visit. These are more likely to be people like your parents or people who are on a social network to see what it's like rather than adopt it into their life.

*More than 30% of Facebook and Twitter users access the sites for less than 30 minutes a day.*

**The Virgins** New people who sign up to social networks may struggle at first with the workings of Facebook and Twitter, but from these beginnings they may go on to become Ultras! You'll spot the virgins right away as they worry about making mistakes or get the social network etiquette wrong (more on this later), for example forgetting they are posting a status update instead of a private message.

*More than 1.7 million people in the UK signed up to Facebook in 2012.*

**The Lurkers** These users rarely participate in social media conversations, either because they don't think they have anything interesting to say or because they just like to observe! You'll know these people because they try to friend everyone but when you look at their pages just the bare bones are there. On some social networks, such as LinkedIn, they can be spotted because these networks tell you who's looking at your page.

*In the survey, 45% of Facebook users described themselves as 'observers', compared to 39% of Twitter users.*

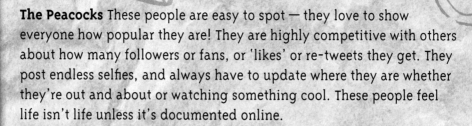

**The Peacocks** These people are easy to spot — they love to show everyone how popular they are! They are highly competitive with others about how many followers or fans, or 'likes' or re-tweets they get. They post endless selfies, and always have to update where they are whether they're out and about or watching something cool. These people feel life isn't life unless it's documented online.

*More than one in ten (11%) of Twitter users say it is important for them to have more 'followers' on their feed than their friends.*

**The Ranters** However timid they may be in face-to-face conversation, ranters are highly opinionated online. Social media allows them to broadcast strong opinions without the worry of how others might react. These are the people who don't really understand why their online behaviour puts people off and why people unfriend or block them.

*11% of Facebook users and 17% of Twitter users say the networks allow them to be more opinionated than they are otherwise.*

**The Ghosts** Some people who use social media worry about giving out personal information to strangers, so they create usernames to stay anonymous or create almost bare profiles and timelines or closed accounts that few others can access.

*'Security' is given as a reason for not using their real names by 15% of Twitter users and 6% of Facebook users.*

**The Changelings** Some people like to create completely different personalities for themselves online. It gives them confidence that no one knows who they really are.

*Around 5% of Facebook and Twitter users say hiding their identities in social media allows them more freedom to say what they really think.*

**The Quizzers** 'Quizzers' like to ask questions on Facebook and Twitter. They enjoy starting conversations and don't want to feel left out.

*According to the survey, around one in ten Facebook and Twitter users say they enjoy using their pages to ask questions, rather than just posting messages or updates.*

**The Informers** Being the first to notice something interesting and share it on social media earns people respect and more followers.

*One in five (20%) of Twitter users and 22% of Facebook users say they like to share information and links with their friends and followers.*

**The Approval-seekers** These people worry about how many likes/comments/re-tweets they get, and link this approval to popularity. They're constantly checking their feeds and timelines.

*One in seven (14%) of Facebook users say it is important that others 'like' or reply to their updates, while 9% of Twitter users say replies and re-tweets are important.*

# REALITY CHECK

## OFFICIAL REALITY CHECKER

THIS CARD CERTIFIES THAT

_ _ _ Melvin _ _ _

IS OFFICIALLY APPOINTED TO CHECK REALITY ON BEHALF OF THE QUICK EXPERT'S GUIDE

APPROVED

☑ **WORLD'S MOST FOLLOWED ON TWITTER**

**Katy Perry**
46 million followers

**Justin Bieber**
46 million followers

**Lady Gaga**
40 million followers

**Barack Obama**
39 million followers

**Taylor Swift**
36 million followers

**YouTube** 35 million followers

**Britney Spears**
33 million followers

**Rihanna** 32 million followers

**Instagram**
28 million followers

**Justin Timberlake**
28 million followers

# * HOW DO I START ON SOCIAL NETWORKS?

Although every site has its own rules, they all work in the same fundamental way. You sign up using your personal details, a user page is then created where you put some basic information about yourself and a photo (it doesn't have to be you but it helps to be you if you want people to find you) and then you're all ready to go.

Once you're all signed up the next step is to get friends (also called followers) to link to your page so you can start having conversations. On Facebook these tend to be friends, family, friends of friends and in some cases complete strangers (never a great idea for safety reasons). On Twitter you start by following people you like — celebrities, TV people, your friends and family, singers, actors anyone you can think of really — and once you start tweeting (sending out updates) people start to follow you.

Twitter works a bit differently from Facebook in that you can follow people and see what they are saying but they don't have to follow you back. This means you can say, send a message to Justin Bieber on his Twitter page, but can't send him a direct private message unless he is following you and vice versa. On Facebook if you've set your privacy settings correctly (more on this later) people can only see your page if you're friends with them and can only post on your page and message you privately if you are 'friends on Facebook' with them.

## SAY WHAT?

Facebook CEO Mark Zuckerberg has amassed 282,000 followers on Twitter despite the fact that he's only tweeted 19 times in four years.

Of course, other social networks work slightly differently, so check out the settings to ensure that you haven't opened up your private world to the whole world before you start posting. Also, you need to be patient — it takes time to build a following and friendship circle. It's not a race to see who can get the most followers.

## ✳ HOW DO I GET PEOPLE TO FOLLOW ME ON SOCIAL NETWORKS?

This really depends on the site you're on. With Facebook you start by sending friend requests to everyone you know and they accept them. This then starts a domino effect — people see that you're on Facebook and start sending you friend requests.

On Twitter it works differently — you start following people you know and are interested in and some will follow you back. However, on Twitter the way to get more followers is to tweet about interesting things and get involved in Twitter conversations. This then highlights you as someone 'interesting' to follow.

On LinkedIn you can only friend people you know as you have to mark how you know them in your request to them. In contrast, on Pinterest and Instagram you can basically choose to follow people based on their pages and pictures/boards.

There are other ways to ensure your page is popular and that's to:

**Share frequently.** People are more likely to want to follow/friend you if they see your page is active, and updated regularly.

**Don't be negative.** Studies show those who post positive updates and fun stories tend to have more followers.

**Be responsive.** That means answer those who ask you questions, send you messages or start following you. Again this makes people see you're an active social networker.

**Use a good picture on your profile page.** Believe it or not, there are lots of people with your name! So if someone is looking for you and all they see is a cartoon shot of Bart or Lisa Simpson they probably won't think it's you.

**Be informative.** As in, don't just post rubbish or selfies! Give people something to come back for so that they'll tell others.

**Get involved.** Being a voice for the issues you feel strongly about and getting involved in relevant conversations is another good way to up your followers and find like-minded souls.

# REALITY CHECK

**OFFICIAL REALITY CHECKER**

THIS CARD CERTIFIES THAT
_ _ _ Melvin _ _ _
IS OFFICIALLY APPOINTED TO CHECK REALITY ON BEHALF OF THE QUICK EXPERT'S GUIDE

APPROVED

☑ Research from Microsoft has found that, as well as using social networking services for entertainment, people also use them to find practical information. Half of those surveyed said they have used their status messages to ask a question and find an answer.

Examples ranged from jokey —
"Why are boys/girls stupid?"

to the practical —
"I smashed my iPhone how do I replace the glass?"

# WHAT CAN I DO ON SOCIAL NETWORKS?

\*DIY DUDE\*
You can do it all!

※ These days it's more of a question of what can't you do on social networks, but here's a list of what you can do:

**Post updates about yourself**

Share photos

**Share video**

Share content on your page from the internet, papers, magazines

**Comment on other people's updates and photos**

**Tag pictures – put up a photo and link to all the friends who are in it**

Get involved with causes you feel strongly about

**Play games**

**Do polls**

Post jokes

**Meet new people**

**Find old friends**

Chat

**Join interest groups**

**Add music**

Give advice

**Get advice**

**Help others**

Send invitations

**Organise events**

Find a job

Ask questions

Dude!

# ✳ SHOULD I BE AFRAID OF SOCIAL NETWORKS?

If you read the papers and have heard some horror stories you might well feel afraid of social media. In the last year alone they've been blamed for a rise in bullying, teen suicide, eating disorders, teens being nasty, teens failing exams, teens becoming depressed and teens forgetting how to be social. In reality social networking sites are easy targets for blame. While they do have their problems (see chapter 5 for more on this), they are not wholly responsible for the on and offline behaviour of users or the woes of the world. So in a nutshell you do not need to be afraid of social networks but you do need to be careful about what you do on them.

In fact, none of us should use social networks without thinking about what we're doing. A social network is a bit like standing on a stage in front of the entire world. You may not think there's anyone watching or listening but there is. And many of those users are what's known as active users, people who are going to share the information you post, come back at you with a comment or simply say something belligerent just for the sake of it (for more on this see Chapter 5).

What you have to do is:

**Be careful what you say.** Always ask yourself: *Do I really want the whole world to know this?* And as part of this general rule:

**Be careful what you say about others.** So you think the ugly picture of your friend is funny but will she once everyone she knows sees it?

**Be careful what you say about yourself.** It may feel right to post a status update about being depressed but again do you want the whole world to make a drama out of this?

**Be careful what you upload.** Do you want everyone at school to see your private pictures and videos?

Remember you're linked to everyone. Always remember when you post on a networking site it's not just going to the few friends who always talk online to you but to EVERYONE. Your mum, family friends, friends of friends etc. in fact anyone who is connected to anyone who is connected to you.

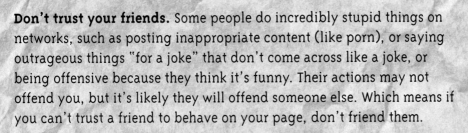

81% of teens aged 12–17 say they use social media sites. Facebook is the most heavily used site with 94% of teens saying they have a profile there.

**SAY WHAT?**

**Don't trust your friends.** Some people do incredibly stupid things on networks, such as posting inappropriate content (like porn), or saying outrageous things "for a joke" that don't come across like a joke, or being offensive because they think it's funny. Their actions may not offend you, but it's likely they will offend someone else. Which means if you can't trust a friend to behave on your page, don't friend them.

**Keep your password private.** As obvious as this sounds, lots of people tell their friends what their password is. This is bad news because it means they can access your page and say things as if they were you, without you knowing (for more on this see Chapter 3).

# ✳ WHAT DO SOCIAL NETWORKS WANT ME TO DO?

All social networks want you to interact and use their site as much as possible. Which is why they are designed to make you feel as if you can't live without being a member and that you're missing out when you're not being active on them.

Much of this is down to the way these sites make money. The common way for networks to generate revenue is to allow companies to advertise on them. The more popular the networking site, the more money it will be able to generate through advertising. Facebook has millions of active users, uploading an immense amount of personal information, so advertisers are willing to pay more for an ad on Facebook than on another social network site.

You may also find some networking sites (the smaller ones and the more professional job-based sites) charge a membership fee to users. For instance LinkedIn can be used free but key features aren't made available to users unless they choose to upgrade to a premium account.

## SAY WHAT?

Every sixty seconds, 293,000 status updates are posted on Facebook.

# ✳ IS SOCIAL NETWORKING ADDICTIVE?

Social networking is meant to be a fun social encounter. A bit like going to a party, talking to lots of people and then leaving. The problem is, the non-stop stream of messages, photos, updates and information coming from those in each network leads many to feel they can never switch off. This doesn't mean that it's addictive but many people do feel a compulsion to constantly check their social network. Studies have shown that a large number of teens check in every few minutes because they are anxious not to miss out on something in their social world. This is because for many teens (and adults) social media is not just a part of their life, it is the hub of their life.

# QUICK EXPERT SUMMARY

- Most people you know are on social networks. Be interesting and they'll connect to you.

- Social networks are not bad, but the behaviour of some people on the networks means you do have to be careful.

- Social networks want you to share and encourage you to share all aspects of your life from personal info to pictures.

- You can use social networks to connect with everyone from a long-lost relative to a famous person.

- Social networking can become a compulsion if you let it.

# SAFE SOCIAL NETWORKING
# BE SMART, BE SAFE

## ✴ AGE RESTRICTIONS ON SOCIAL NETWORKS

While social networking is at its heart something fun that allows you to communicate easily with friends and family, most social networks have an age restriction. The main reason for this is that many of these companies are American and in the USA there is a children's online privacy law that prevents a child's personal information being collected and shared. This includes their geo location, photos and video. However, the age restriction on networks is also there because social networks are made for adults and so the content being shared and spoken about is adult based. This means if you are under 13 you are unlikely to have the experience or the reasoning needed to handle what's being shared.

That said, a huge number of under-13s are on social media sites (by lying about their age) and experts believe it's the reason why pre-teens are also increasingly becoming victims of online harassment, online grooming (where sexual predators target teens and win their trust) and cyber-bullying.

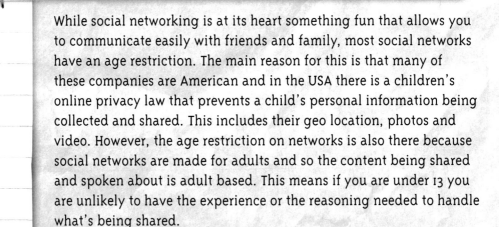

SAY WHAT?

Over one third of 9- to 12-year-olds have Facebook accounts.

If you're thinking about lying about your
age to get a social network account here are
some things to consider:

**1. Could you handle malicious and
nasty comments that sometimes
occur?** Unfortunately social networking
makes some people behave in a way
they would not in person. Trolls are people who can be horrible, say
mean things and generally make your online life miserable.

**2. Could you handle age-inappropriate content such as violent
images?** The internet provides access to all kinds of content but not
all of that content is suitable for young people to see. While you may
think you're in control of what you're seeing — you're not. Anyone
you're connected to can post anything on your timeline/page/wall.

**3. Could you spot if someone had a fake profile?** People sometimes
aren't what they seem. Anyone can set up a fake social network
account and friend you (if you let them). They may sound and look
like a 14-year-old boy or girl but in reality they could be anyone.

**4. Would you know what to do if something scary happened?** Who
would you turn to for help, advice and support? While it's easy to
believe nothing will ever scare you online, there is a lot out there that
scares even adults.

Even if you're on a social network that does not have an age
restriction, it's worth checking out if you're ready for it or not by
looking at someone else's account first and thinking about privacy
and the settings around your profile (for more on this see below).

# ✳ PRIVACY AND PRIVACY SETTINGS

Many adults, never mind teens, do not understand the risks involved
in giving out too much personal information on social networks.
Aside from the fact that anyone accessing your site can gather
the information you give out, everything you say and do online is

information. If you're connected to people you don't actually know, what you're doing is saying: *This is what I look like, this is where I live, this is what I like, this is my best friend's name and this is where I am right now.* That's scary when you think about it because in connecting to strangers you've basically told them how to get to know you and find you quickly.

Part of the problem with privacy is that, to many people, the online world isn't the same as the real world, and so they often behave online in a way they would never do in the real world. For starters people are less protective of personal data details such as their address, their age and even their phone number.

Studies do show that when it comes to privacy online, teens are the least concerned, with less than 10% worrying about it. However, it's very important to think about who can see your content and what information you're posting. For instance, if you're on a social network is your page set to private and only visible to 'friends'? One fifth of teens still leave their profiles set to public so everyone can see everything, including being able to look through photo albums and copy pictures.

**SAY WHAT?** One third of Facebook users readily admit they don't actually know all their 'friends'.

Privacy is also about protecting you from yourself. We all leave what's known as a digital footprint, which means a history of everything we've ever posted online. This may not bother you right now but your content (pictures, videos, written posts) has long-term implications for everything from college applications to jobs. Posting rude and embarrassing content will not be so funny when a prospective employer looks you up on Google further down the line. With privacy settings set to 'friends only' you can limit the potential future damage.

In a recent survey 57% of teens said they had decided not to post something online because they were concerned it would reflect badly on them in the future.

**SAY WHAT?**

***DIY DUDE***

Privacy settings

The easy way to deal with these privacy issues is to take a look at your privacy settings and set them to protect your information and content. Bear in mind that these settings will be different on every site and that they change regularly. Social networks will tell you when their settings have changed and this allows you to keep a close eye on what's happening with your accounts. For instance on Twitter when you protect your tweets, the following restrictions are put in place:

People will have to request to follow you; each follow request will need approval from you.

Dude!

- Your tweets will only be visible to users you've approved.

- Other users will not be able to re-tweet your tweets.

- Protected tweets will not appear in Google search.

- You cannot share links to your tweets with anyone other than your approved followers.

If you like taking part in lively debates and use Twitter to have conversations with many people this may not be the right privacy choice for you, but only you can say.

*instagram.com*

On **Instagram** you can set your photos and videos to private so that only approved followers can see them. Bear in mind that if you then share a photo to another social network (such as Twitter, Facebook, Foursquare, etc.) using Instagram, the image will be visible on that network and accessible by anyone on that network. On YouTube when you upload a video, by default it's set as a 'Public' video, which means that anybody can view it. However, you can easily change the privacy settings while you're uploading the video in the 'Privacy Settings' section to private or unlisted. Unlisted videos are private videos that anyone can view if, and only if, they have access to the video's URL. These videos will not show up on public pages, in search results or on user channels.

**\*DIY DUDE\***
Setting privacy controls on Facebook

1. **Click on the privacy control icon** (like a small wheel) in the upper right of your Facebook home screen. Then click 'Privacy Settings and Account Settings'. It's here that you can control who sees your content and who can access your page.

2. **To protect who sees your page and content** go to 'Who can see my stuff' section. In the drop-down menu, click 'Custom'. If you want to keep it simple, you can opt to share only with friends or friends of friends.

3. **To protect what goes on your page** go to the Timeline and Tagging Settings and click 'on' to the Review posts friends tag you in before they appear on your timeline. This ensures no pictures or offensive posts can appear with you tagged in without your consent.

4. **To get rid of people you don't want to share your online space with,** go to Manage Blocking. This is where you block people who annoy/ irritate or post horrible things on your timeline. Once you block someone, that person can no longer see things you post on your timeline, tag you, invite you to events or groups, start a conversation with you, or add you as a friend.

Dude!

**SAY WHAT?**

# THE IMPORTANCE OF USERNAMES AND PASSWORDS

How do you choose your password? Is it your name? Is it your date of birth? Would someone be able to guess it easily? If you're like most people the answer is probably yes to all three of those. The truth is, on the whole most of us create ridiculously easy-to-guess passwords. A major study on passwords and how we choose them shows:

14% of passwords are derived from people's names, and of those, 42% add their birthdate to make it seem complicated e.g. Jack14.

25% of passwords are derived from dictionary words, with 'password', 'monkey' and 'dragon' being the top three favourites.

14% of passwords are numeric with '123456', '12345678' and '123456789' being the top three picks!

8% are from place names, specifically the city someone lives in.

Only 1% of passwords are random.

The obvious answer here is if you want to create a strong password choose something long, random (as in it has no link to you), unique and possibly, if the site lets you, include symbols.

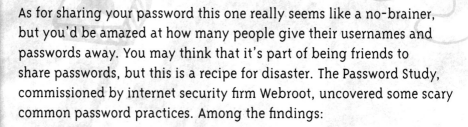

As for sharing your password this one really seems like a no-brainer, but you'd be amazed at how many people give their usernames and passwords away. You may think that it's part of being friends to share passwords, but this is a recipe for disaster. The Password Study, commissioned by internet security firm Webroot, uncovered some scary common password practices. Among the findings:

4 in 10 respondents said they'd shared passwords with at least one person in the past year.

Almost as many people use the same password to log into multiple websites, risking the exposure of their information on each of the sites if one of them were to become compromised.

2 in 10 admitted using a significant date, such as their birthday, or a pet's name as a password — information that's often publicly visible on social networks.

12 per cent of young people said they'd shared a password in a text message.

Over half of young people surveyed said they'd shared passwords with one or more other people in the past year.

So here's a scenario for you on why you shouldn't give your password away: You give your best friend your Facebook password because you're not home and you want her to check something for you. Two months down the line you've fallen out and she now has access to your account and can log in and say whatever she likes under your name. Now you have a compromised profile, and if you link to other sites or profiles, all that information is at risk as well. The solution is to **keep your password to yourself**, no matter what.

Whenever you're using other people's devices and public computers, remember to log off from your social networks before you go. Otherwise your page is vulnerable to other people's nosiness — and even to abuse.

# ✳ WHO ARE YOU CONNECTING TO?

98% of Facebook-using teens are friends with people they know from school. 89% are connected to friends who do not attend the same school. 33% are Facebook friends with other people they have not met in person.

**SAY WHAT?**

Part of the problem with social media is that it can feel like a competition to see how many likes, friends and followers you can get. As a result it's easy to accept invitations from anyone who asks, or ask people you don't know to friend you. Of course part of the appeal of social networks is the chance to network (or communicate) with friends, friends of friends, and friends of those friends. However, even friends of friends are strangers if you think about it. And complete strangers who look good on their profiles and sound nice are people you probably shouldn't let into your world. Anyone can create a fake profile and pretend to be someone they're not and even if they are real, by accepting invites from people you don't know you're opening up your page (and your life) to a whole network of strangers.

Even Facebook suggests that "*You should send friend requests to people you have a real-life connection to, like your friends, family or classmates. If you're interested in receiving updates from people you find interesting, but don't know personally (e.g. journalists, celebrities, political figures), try following them instead of sending them friend requests.*" This will allow you to see the public updates in News Feed from people you're interested in but aren't friends with.

In terms of who you're connecting to, it does of course depend on the social network you're on. On Twitter, for example, anyone can follow you but they cannot send you a direct message (private message) unless you follow them back. This means you have the option to be very careful about who you let into your account.

# ✳ TO SHARE OR NOT TO SHARE?

Another factor to consider is what you are sharing online. This is as important as privacy in that content (and we'll see more about this in chapter 4) is what gets people into trouble on social networks. One simple factor to consider when getting onto a network is to think about the personal information that you're allowing everyone to see.

When you sign up to most networks you have to key in a lot of information and, unless you read the small print, this content can easily be displayed on your profile page.

## REALITY CHECK

**OFFICIAL REALITY CHECKER**

THIS CARD CERTIFIES THAT

_ _ _ Melvin _ _ _

IS OFFICIALLY APPOINTED TO CHECK REALITY ON BEHALF OF THE QUICK EXPERT'S GUIDE

APPROVED

☑ **WHAT TEENS SHARE ON FACEBOOK**

91% post a photo of themselves

82% post their birth date

71% post the name of their school

71% post the city or town where they live

53% post their email address

20% post their phone number

Think carefully about what needs to be given away and what doesn't. A photo and city you live in is okay, but posting your phone number and school name isn't.

Also think about all the information you give away when you take part in those fun quizzes and polls that everyone shares. Bear in mind that something you think is private can easily be shared and then shared again, and be out there for the whole world to see.

A few quick words about over-sharing — that's giving out too much information about your life, views and feelings and bombarding friends and followers with your updates. Firstly, while you may be off-loading and don't mean half of what you say, the content you post online sticks in people's minds and can easily be taken out of context. Think before you share!

Secondly, think about how often you post. You may be posting because you have a lot to say or because you're bored, but think about the impact of the number of your posts on others. It may be better to IM via What'sApp or a private message rather than telling everyone with a status update.

# QUICK EXPERT SUMMARY

- Pay attention to age restrictions – they are there to stop you seeing harmful content.

- Always check out the privacy settings – they are there to protect your privacy and restrict who can gain access to your information.

- Passwords are easy to guess so be smart about choosing one – make it long, random and complicated.

- Be selective – don't connect to everyone and their dog. Social networking is not a competition.

- Don't share personal information on your profile. It makes it too easy for people to invade your real world.

# SMART CONTENT

## * WHAT IS CONTENT?

Content in a nutshell is all the stuff on your social network page. It isn't just words these days, it's anything you post — from pictures to videos, to status updates, to jokes, to polls, to news stories. It's the fuel that drives social networks and without it we'd all be off doing something else. Some people believe it's this need or desire for information about and from others that drives us all to be on social networks. We all want to know what our friends are up to — we're curious about what they did at the weekend, what they wore, who they saw, what they think and whether they're happy or not.

Social networks like Facebook and Twitter have made it possible to know this information, which in the past would typically have been kept private or given in a face-to-face way only. So for instance, you can now see other people's holiday pictures, photos of someone's new cousin or hear news that X has broken up with Y within minutes of it happening, all thanks to the content your friends and followers are posting.

## * WHY DO WE POST CONTENT?

It sounds weird to say it, but at the heart of social networking is the fact that we all like to talk about ourselves. Don't worry, this doesn't meant that we're super egotistical, but more that it's a human need to express ourselves and be given feedback from people we like and love.

Social networks allow you to do this in an easy and non-threatening way. On Twitter, for instance, you can post content that gives your personal view of a TV show and, by using the hashtag # symbol, join a conversation with thousands of other people who feel the same way as you. This lets you feel you are correct in your outrage or joy at something. On Facebook simply posting a picture of your new haircut or photos of yourself on holiday can give you a huge return of satisfaction in terms of comments, compliments and likes.

*So why do we share?*

*One Harvard University study found that talking about yourself gives you the same pleasure kick as food and love.*

## ✳ WHAT ARE YOU POSTING AND WHY?

The problem with social media is the very thing we love the most — content. Due to the fact that we can pretty much say what we want and in any way we want and with any type of media (photos, videos, live streaming) there is a lot of space for things to go wrong. The following are all examples of content that can be put up in good faith that can cause problems:

✳ Posting a video/picture that offends people.

✳ Tagging friends in photos that they don't want to be made public.

✳ Saying something on your profile that should have been put in a private message.

✳ Talking about someone you forget you're linked to.

✳ Saying something that others find offensive.

✳ Commenting on content that then upsets someone else.

The fact to remember is that social networks are very public spaces, which means, although you may think you're just talking to your best friends, you're not. What you're posting is going out (depending on your settings) to friends, friends of friends, and strangers. So before you post always think: *Will this offend anyone?* And most important of all: *Would I show this or say this face-to-face to my friends?* If you wouldn't then don't post it.

Secondly, if you are about to post something inflammatory, think about why you're posting it. Is it to get a reaction? Is it because you're mad at someone? Or are you looking for reassurance? Whatever the reason, bear in mind that, whether you think they do or not, online actions have consequences. Although you may be able to delete a post later, you have little control over older versions that may exist on other people's devices and may be circulating online.

Thirdly, there is some information about yourself, your friends and your family that should be kept private: details such as your address and phone number, but also personal information that you wouldn't stand and shout about in the playground or print in a newspaper. This is the stuff you should not include in your posts.

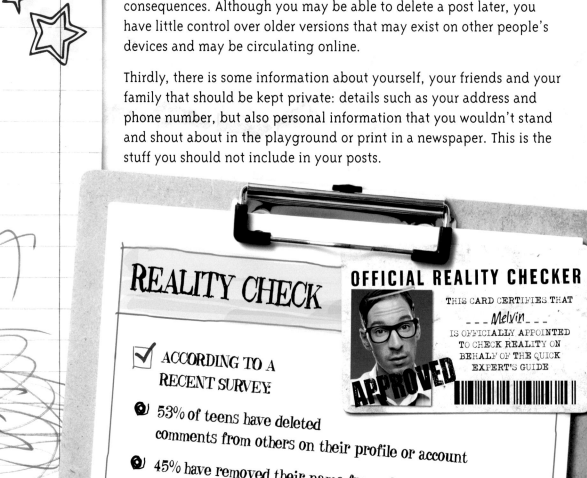

## REALITY CHECK

**OFFICIAL REALITY CHECKER**

THIS CARD CERTIFIES THAT

_ _ _ Melvin _ _ _

IS OFFICIALLY APPOINTED TO CHECK REALITY ON BEHALF OF THE QUICK EXPERT'S GUIDE

APPROVED

☑ **ACCORDING TO A RECENT SURVEY:**

👁 53% of teens have deleted comments from others on their profile or account

👁 45% have removed their name from photos that have been tagged to identify them

👁 19% have posted updates, comments, photos or videos that they later regretted sharing

## ✳ TEXT AS CONTENT

The things you say are 'content' as much as anything else, and this is the area that gets most people into trouble. Often it's down to the simple fact that people forget that they are sharing with the whole world. Take the case of the driver who tweeted that she had knocked a cyclist off his bike and left him there. She obviously tweeted it for her friends' benefit, yet the whole world saw her tweet, including said cyclist and the police who arrested her. The answer (aside from not doing criminal things) is to think before you post something, asking yourself if what you're about to say will cause upset or hurt or get you into trouble.

## ✳ PHOTO SHARING

Each day 300 million photos are added to Facebook.

SAY WHAT?

Who doesn't love seeing other people's pictures? Holiday snaps, selfies, group pictures and funny pictures. Photos feed our love of social networks in a way that other content doesn't. However, posting pictures can sometimes cause huge problems. For a start many people think posting horrible pictures of friends for everyone to see is funny. Known as tagging, this is where you tag in other people's names when you post so the said picture automatically appears on their feed/pages as well as yours. While it might be funny for you and some of your friends, doing this can really upset others. So think about how you would feel before you post something.

Lots of people also love to post horrible images. In this sense horrible can mean sick, violent, pornographic or just revolting. Like anything it's worth bearing in mind that horrible pictures can really upset people, so if you wouldn't show a picture like this to your friend or your mum do not post it online.

Lastly, bear in mind some images are plain stupid to post online. Pictures showing you participating in an illegal activity (think about the celebrities who post pictures of themselves with drugs) or semi-nude pictures are just asking for trouble. Likewise, pictures of you or friends naked or drunk should be avoided at all costs.

# REALITY CHECK

**OFFICIAL REALITY CHECKER**

THIS CARD CERTIFIES THAT
_ _ _ *Melvin* _ _ _
IS OFFICIALLY APPOINTED TO CHECK REALITY ON BEHALF OF THE QUICK EXPERT'S GUIDE

APPROVED

 ☑ INAPPROPRIATE OR ILLEGAL CONTENT

In a recent survey of social media users, 54% said they had received an 'inappropriate picture', 47% had received nude pictures and a further 11% claimed to have seen images of 'criminal acts'.

Teenage girls are more likely to send semi-nude or nude photos of themselves than boys (22% vs 18%), and 12% of those surveyed recently in a US questionnaire stated that they sent pictures because they were 'pressured into it'.

And let's talk about selfies — the celebrity-driven need to post a picture of yourself looking cool. Again these are harmless unless you start posting a lot, as this can attract negative attention. What's more, think about how you're posing in these pictures (the current trend is to make selfies sexy) and what you are and aren't wearing. All these things can attract the wrong kind of

online attention (for more on this see Chapter 5). The rule is, if you wouldn't show it round the dinner table, don't show it online.

# ✳ VIDEO

Video is one of the most shared pieces of content on social networks (Facebook users alone watch more than 500 years' worth of YouTube video every day). Sharing music videos, clips from TV shows, films and funny 'You've Been Framed'-style clips is usually not problematic. Again though, think about what you're sharing before you share. One person's funny is another's offensive. Videos that feature naked people, violent images and sick images offend and upset a lot of people and can get you into trouble. Also, think about personal videos you've taken with your smart phone. Sharing videos of your friend doing something embarrassing isn't funny to your friend. Likewise, sharing videos of something criminal or cruel will get you more attention then you bargained for, especially if you post on YouTube.

Currently YouTube is used as a social network as well as a viewing site. As a result there are more than 1 billion YouTube views per day on mobile devices alone and YouTube users watch, comment on and share more than 6 billion hours of video on the site each month (and let's not even get into Vine and Tumblr). That's an awful lot of video, so think twice before you post something embarrassing of yourself or others. It won't go away and will be there even years from now when someone searches online for you.

## SAY WHAT?

4.8 million Facebook users share about leaving the house.

Location-based social networking is now huge, and whereas only a few years ago people were up in arms about it, now most of us have embraced it. Most location-based networks focus on 'checking in' at various locations to earn points, badges, discounts and other geo related awards. Foursquare (which has 40 million users), for instance, is a location-based social networking website for mobile devices. Users 'check-in' at various places using a mobile website and are then awarded points. Users can also connect and publish their 'check ins' to Facebook and Twitter.

## REALITY CHECK

**OFFICIAL REALITY CHECKER**

THIS CARD CERTIFIES THAT
_ _ _ Melvin _ _ _
IS OFFICIALLY APPOINTED TO CHECK REALITY ON BEHALF OF THE QUICK EXPERT'S GUIDE

APPROVED

☑ **BURGLARS**

Almost four in five (78%) of ex-burglars interviewed in the UK believe that thieves use social media sites to identify targets. Bad news when 35% of 18-34-year-olds check in or tweet about their current location when they're away from home!

Facebook's 'places' button works in a similar way to Foursquare in that you can post exactly where you are when you're out and about. However it gives an individual's location when the user posts information using a mobile device. This function is automatically active on all Facebook accounts until it is disabled.

Unless you want everyone to know where you are 24/7, sharing your social plans for everybody to see isn't a good idea. If you tell everyone you're going on a date, for example, any number people could turn up and spoil it. Most of all, telling people where you are all the time and where you live, does leave you exposed when you don't have to be. Geo-tag responsibly and check your settings.

> The Quick Expert was careful with his settings when he went on a date, but the rose was a bit of a giveaway.

# QUICK EXPERT SUMMARY

- Content is not just words, it's video, photos, news stories, live streaming and more.

- Content can often offend people and get you into trouble, so think before you post or share anything.

- Geo-tagging is everywhere and enables people to know where you are 24/7. Check your settings before you post.

- On the whole, content is now integrated, which means that if you belong to two social networks or more, what you post is likely to appear in both places.

- Online content sharing has long-term consequences because even if you delete something, it can still exist on other pages, especially if it's been shared.

# Chapter 5

# THE RISKS AND HOW TO HANDLE THEM

## ✳ WHAT ARE THE RISKS OF SOCIAL NETWORKING?

There are risks to everything we do in life, and social networking is no different. Being on a network, you risk meeting the wrong person, falling out with the people you know online, being lied to, being misunderstood, having someone post mean stuff about you, being bullied... the list is endless. And while there are some obvious ways to

protect yourself, such as not 'befriending' people you don't know and managing your privacy settings, sometimes not-so-nice things happen.

When they do it's important to act, as online problems linked to your offline life have a way of exploding. Recently there were tragic consequences to a bullying attack on the social network Ask.fm and also on Facebook. The key here is to shut down nasty things that happen as fast as you can with help from others. This chapter shows you how to resolve some of these issues, but it doesn't mean you have to avoid social networks or that they are a bad thing. In reality you simply have to learn how to manage your online life in the same way as you manage your offline life.

# SOCIAL MEDIA ETIQUETTE

To avoid being misunderstood online there are some essential etiquette points to bear in mind. Firstly, talking to someone on social media isn't the same as talking in person. Much of how we communicate is via body language and tone of voice, so the written word on its own often won't convey our true meaning. This can mean that the things we say as a joke sometimes don't come across as funny, and the responses we mean to have empathy can sound hard and uncaring.

Another thing that happens online is that we can say things without stopping to think about the effect they may have. This happens because the person we're talking to isn't right in front of us. So for instance, we don't think before we comment negatively on a friend's new haircut, when in person we'd never dare to say "It looks terrible." Social media is full of this kind of thoughtlessness, especially when people post their photos and personal thoughts. Likewise, many people lose perspective on their emotions, get overly angry or lash out with hurtful responses when they feel they have been wronged or something annoys them. It's for this reason that social media etiquette is so important.

**Be respectful in your comments.** Do not say anything online that you wouldn't say face-to-face.

**Don't be overly sensitive.** It's easy to misinterpret what people say, so don't be so quick to take offense and get angry. Speak to the person and clarify what has happened before responding online.

**DON'T SPEAK IN CAPITALS TO MAKE YOUR POINT!** It's like shouting in someone's face and it upsets people.

**If you say something that could be misinterpreted, use an emoticon** (smiley face/sad face) to convey your intended meaning.

**Ask before you post a pic of someone.** Many people don't like being tagged in pictures or having private pictures of themselves posted online.

## ✳ CYBER BULLYING

SAY WHAT?

88% of teens said they have witnessed people being mean and cruel to others on social networking sites. 15% say they have been the target of cyber bullying.

A problem with social networks is that they make cyber bullying all too easy, and unlike in real life the bullying often takes a nastier turn because it starts to happen all the time, wherever you are — even in places you should be able to feel safe like your home. Plus, because of its very nature, what starts off as one-on-one abuse can potentially end up involving large numbers of people.

For those who suffer cyber bullying, the effects are horrible. It can leave people feeling ashamed, hurt, humiliated, angry, depressed and even suicidal. You may wonder why people who are targeted by cyber bullies don't just log off, but the reality is, cyber bullying is so intrusive and manipulative that it's easy to fall into a trap whereby you can't stop checking the network to see what's happening and what's being said about you.

Cyber bullying can take the form of:

Name-calling and rumour-spreading on someone's social network pages.

Being mean via comments, replies, tags and in posts.

Excluding someone online.

Tagging horrible pictures/videos of someone for all to see.

Sending threatening or nasty messages at all hours on sites, via direct messaging.

Posting nasty sex messages, pictures and sexual name-calling.

Posting photos, personal information or fake comments about someone.

Tricking someone into revealing something personal.

Pretending to be someone online.

Involving others to tease, belittle and call someone names.

**\*DIY DUDE\***

Dealing with bullies

Dude!

If you get into a situation where someone is bullying you on a social network there are actions you can take. Do not keep it a secret — like all forms of bullying, it won't go away on its own. Most importantly, do not blame yourself — bullying is never your fault. To cope on a day-to-day basis try not to retaliate or reply in anger — bullies are looking for a reaction.

Then tell your parents. They can contact the moderator on the relevant social networking site with a complaint. At the same time, make sure you keep everything you are sent and messaged. This is evidence and also a way to track down your bullies. If you know the bullies, block them. You may not want to do this for fear of 'upsetting' them or then not being able to see what they say, but it's a positive step to ending the bullying. On sites that are anonymous, such as Ask.fm, bullies feel they will never be found or held accountable for their actions (which is what fuels their bullying behaviour). This is not true and anyone can be tracked down through his or her ISP (internet service provider) and via the social network for threatening and bullying behaviour.

Bear in mind that it's easier to deal with cyber bullying on the big social networks like Facebook than on the smaller sites such as Little Gossip (a social network that encourages the sharing of gossip and relies on users to act as moderators). You can report someone to Facebook and they will close their account or block someone completely and prevent them from starting conversations with you or seeing things you post on your timeline (though of course this doesn't stop them using other people's accounts).

If you're being bullied across various sites, the best advice is to shut down your activity on all of them until it is sorted out. You will probably not want to do this, but often weaning yourself away from social networks completely for a while can help you to feel as if you have regained control of the situation.

## CYBER BULLYING FACT

The charity Beat Bullying says that one in three young people are the target of cyber bullying, and one in 13 encounter persistent abuse online.

Whatever you decide to do, seek support and help offline. Bullying destroys people's confidence and self esteem and you will need help to get through it.

SAY WHAT?

In one American state you can be arrested for posting visual imagery that has the possibility to "frighten, intimidate or cause emotional distress to anyone who sees it".

# ✳ TROLLS AND TROLLING

## TROLLING FACT

Trolling is a criminal offence. People have recently been jailed for posting offensive messages about women on Instagram and abusive messages to a campaigner on Twitter and for being nasty on Facebook tribute pages.

Sometimes being on a social network makes some people (known as trolls) think that they can say and do anything they want to the people they follow. This can range from being vindictive, nasty and spiteful, to committing criminal offences, such as sending violent threats. Studies show that these trolls are often (but not always) young adult males who do it for amusement, boredom and revenge. The single driving factor behind trolling is the fact that all these people do it because they can stay anonymous or hide behind a fake account (another reason not to welcome people you truly don't know onto your account).

## REALITY CHECK

### OFFICIAL REALITY CHECKER

THIS CARD CERTIFIES THAT
_ _ _ Melvin _ _ _
IS OFFICIALLY APPOINTED
TO CHECK REALITY ON
BEHALF OF THE QUICK
EXPERT'S GUIDE

### ☑ TROLLING

The psychology behind this phenomenon can be found in the term 'troll' itself, which is thought to derive from a fishing technique of slowly dragging a baited hook from a moving boat. 'Trolls' post inflammatory remarks ( the metaphorical 'bait') to illicit a response from those they have abused ( the metaphorical 'fish').

If you know someone who is behaving like a troll, it's worth telling them that under section 127 of The Communications Act 2003 it is an offence to send messages that are "grossly offensive or of an indecent, obscene or menacing character". As for how to deal with trolls who won't leave you alone, the best way is to:

Immediately tell friends and family what's going on — trolls can be frightening and intimidating and even when you have switched off their nasty threats and words can linger.

Report any anonymous abuse or intimidation to the social network you're on or to the moderator of the network, or if it's really serious, contact the police.

Trolls think they are untouchable but they're not — their IP address (where the message came from) can be tracked.

Do not reply or retaliate.

Block all users that send abusive messages (do this in settings).

Of course, sometimes, trolls can be personal friends who like to tease and joke online or try to kick off big online fights just for the fun of it. This kind of troll is easier to deal with — either refuse to be drawn into an argument and delete the said post or tell your friend to cut it out. If friends persist in acting like trolls, block them from your account so they can't comment, post or see your wall.

## ✳ SEXUAL CONTENT ON SOCIAL NETWORKS

One of the main unwanted things you may come across on social networks is pornography. The key here again is to set your privacy settings, don't friend people you don't know and take action when one of your friends posts something you find offensive. This could mean telling them to stop, or blocking them completely.

Unknown 'friends' and 'followers' can also start sending you explicit images or content and asking you to share images with them. If this is happening to you, report it right away.

# A LITTLE MORE ON SELFIES ON SOCIAL NETWORKS

Selfies are pictures people take of themselves by holding a smartphone at arm's length and adopting a pose. The selfie is then posted to social networking sites. The problem with selfies is that (1) they encourage you to adopt a sexy pose when taking the pic and (2) they can easily be copied and end up all over the internet. Plus, if you keep posing pics in an overtly sexual way, all you're doing is attracting that kind of attention back. Like most things on social networks, less is more.

# WEBCAM USE ON NETWORKS

Some social networks allow you to chat to people online that you know and don't know. Webcam chats are becoming more common and, if you're tempted to chat via webcam, there are some things to bear in mind. As we've said before, people lie on social networking sites and some want to chat to you on webcam so they can video you doing things you wouldn't ordinarily do or ask you to send them sexy pictures. You may think this will never happen to you but it has happened to hundreds of teens who are coaxed, groomed, flattered and bullied into doing it.

Part of the reason is that it's very easy to get carried away on webcam and forget what you're doing, especially as it feels private. The reality is, what happens on a webcam can be recorded and used against you on social networks, and once this has happened it's hard to stop it. If you've had something like this happen to you, or if it's still happening, tell someone you trust like Childline 0800 IIII, your parents and **CEOP**, the Child Exploitation and Online Protection Centre.

http://ceop.police.uk/

## ✳ BE AWARE OF ONLINE GROOMING

Online grooming is when an adult or older person forms a relationship with a teen or younger person with the intent of later having sexual contact or committing other crimes. This can take place via instant messaging, social networking sites and email. Again, you may think it will never happen to you but it does happen, to hundreds of young people.

It starts with online chat on your networking page that can appear innocent, but always involves some level of deception, such as the adult pretending to be someone else (a younger boy or girl or a fan of a group you like). They then attempt to establish a relationship to gain your trust, such as using the information on your network to make you think you have the same interests and feelings about things. They also flatter and compliment excessively. All these tactics can lead you to believe that this person completely understands you. After your trust develops the groomer may start to private message you and then will start to use sexually explicit conversations to test boundaries, lower your inhibitions and use their power to get you to do what they want.

If you feel at all uneasy about a conversation or online relationship you have on a social network, block the person instantly and tell an adult what's going on.

## ✳ TIME ONLINE

SAY WHAT?

51% of teens log into social media once a day and 25% of teens log into to social media 10+ times per day.

One of the biggest criticisms of social networks are that they stop people from interacting face-to-face and aren't, in fact, social. The good news is this isn't true. Social networking, especially amongst teens, doesn't compete but complements face-to-face socialising, with most young people using it as a way to socialise when they are not together. Studies show that 88% of teens value social media because it helps them keep in touch with friends they don't see often and a third of teens say they feel social networking makes them more outgoing. This is backed up by studies like the one from the University of Chicago, which shows that teens who use social networks to generate and enhance relationships benefit the most from them.

Researchers also claim that being on social networks promotes invaluable skills of social identity and development and enhances skills such as collaboration, communication and technological proficiency. It's probably why over half of teens on social networks claim social networking strengthens their friendships and family relationships and helps them find others with common interests.

# QUICK EXPERT SUMMARY

- Online problems can affect your offline life, so you need to act on them and ask for help and support.

- To avoid being misunderstood online, stop and think before you post an update or a comment and consider how someone will 'read' your words.

- Cyber bullying is an invasive and intrusive form of bullying that you can only stop by telling someone it is happening.

- Trolls are anonymous bullies who think they cannot be traced or stopped – but they can be.

- Never send any sexual images of yourself to anyone. Once they are on a social network they can be copied and posted anywhere.

- Social networking enhances a range of skills from communication to improving your social identity.

# THE LAST WORD ON SAFE SOCIAL NETWORKING

Having **dipped your toe** in the water of social networking, hopefully you can now **go forth** and **love your online life** using whatever piece of equipment you may have. The most important thing to remember is **be safe and have fun!**

# Useful links

**Bullying/Cyberbullying** http://www.bullying.co.uk/

**Centre For Internet Addiction** http://www.netaddiction.com/

**ChatDanger** http://www.chatdanger.com/
- how to stay safe while chatting online

**Child Exploitation and Online Protection Centre** http://ceop.police.uk/

**Childine** http://www.childline.org.uk/
http://www.childline.org.uk/explore/bullying/pages/cyberbullying.aspx

**Facebook** http://www.facebook.com/safety

**Internet Safety For Parents** http://internet-safety.yoursphere.com/

**NSPCC** http://www.nspcc.org.uk

**Play Safe (UKIE)** http://www.ukie.org.uk/playsafe

**Safe Kids** http://www.safekids.com/

**Safer Internet** http://www.saferinternet.org.uk/

**Think U Know** http://www.thinkuk now.co.uk/
- how to stay safe online

**active user** — someone who shares and comments on social networks a lot.

**apps** — software programs that you can download to a mobile device or tablet.

**content** — text, photos, videos or shares you add to your personal page on a social network.

**cyber bullying** — bullying that occurs by text, email on social networks or by instant messaging.

**direct message** — a private message sent to you on a social network.

**follower** — someone who follows your tweets on Twitter.

**friend** — someone who is allowed to see your postings on Facebook.

**geo-tagging** — the process of adding geographical identification to your photographs, video, websites and SMS messages. It is the equivalent of adding a location to everything you post on the internet.

**grooming** — the activity of an adult who is trying to win the online trust of a child or young person for sexual means.

**instant messaging** — real time messaging enabled via an app or social network.

**integrated networks** — social network accounts that are linked, with the result that what you do on one account appears on another.

**live streaming** — real time audio or video, rather than pre-recorded content that you download to a computer to listen to or watch later.

**moderator** — somone who checks on the content of a website and responds to complaints about offensive content or bullying behaviour.

**multimedia** – images, video, sound and text.

**post** – content you put up on a social network, or the act of putting up that content.

**privacy policy** – a statement describing how a social network collects and uses information and when and how they might disclose this information to others. Privacy policies vary from network to network.

**privacy settings** – the method of controlling who sees what on your social network profile.

**private message** – same as a direct message.

**selfies** – self-portraits taken holding a smartphone at arm's length.

**sharing** – The passing on of content on social networks.

**social media sites** – transmit, or share information such as music and photos with a broad audience.

**social network** – sites that build relationships through community.

**status update** – content that tells your friends and followers where you are, what you are doing or how you are feeling.

**tags** – when you are linked to a picture being posted on someone else's page. This link will also bring the picture up on your page without your consent (though you can change this in settings).

**timeline** – the information you see when you log on to your network on Facebook.

**trolling** – nasty online behaviour that ranges from making vindictive and spiteful comments to committing a criminal offence, such as sending violent threats.

**tweet** – your postings on Twitter, text-based messages of up to 140 characters each in length.